IN THE WAKE OF THE 'FLOWER OF GLOSTER'

The author was born and educated in London. He was engaged in diagnostic medical physics at two London teaching hospitals before his interests moved to British art and particularly the work of a number of Scottish artists. Following a period in Edinburgh he moved to an area of Gloucestershire within easy reach of the upper Thames and the Oxford, Stratford and Thames & Severn canals.

Also by John Kemplay

The Thames Locks

IN THE WAKE OF THE

'FLOWER OF GLOSTER'

A reconstruction of Temple Thurston's
historic canal journey of 1911

by

John Kemplay

With photographs by the author

RONALD CROWHURST

Gloucestershire

Published by
Ronald Crowhurst & Co
5 West End Terrace
Chipping Campden
Gloucestershire

First Published 2004

ISBN 0 9518964 2 3

British Library Cataloguing-in-Publication Data

A catalogue record for this book is
available from the British Library

Printed by Graham Printing Co., 47A Thistle Street, Edinburgh

To

the memory of
BELLWATTLE

CONTENTS

ILLUSTRATIONS

FOREWORD

Mr E Temple Thurston

Novelist and Dramatist

It has been suggested that sentimentalism was too much in evidence in Temple Thurston's work, but his reply to this criticism was 'that the only realist was the man of sentiment.' Sentiment is however to be found in *The 'Flower of Gloster'*, which is an account of his journey by canal boat and by foot from Oxford to Inglesham using the Oxford, Stratford, and Thames & Severn canals. His journey took place in May of 1911, the year after he and his first wife were divorced. His second marriage was no more successful than the first and it too ended in divorce, but his third wife survived him. There is no mention of an issue from any of the three marriages.

Ernest Temple Thurston was born in 1879; his origins were most likely the south of Ireland. He began his career as a writer in London at the age of sixteen and published two books of poems. There followed several novels of which some are anti-catholic and this is so of his first novel, *The Apple of Eden*, which was published in a rewritten form in 1905 and is about a priest who falls in love. Many of Temple Thurston's novels had a large sale both in England and other parts of the world, but he was also drawn to the theatre and it is likely that the success of one of his plays gave him more pleasure than the success of one of his novels. Of the dozen or more plays he wrote, *The Wandering Jew* (1920) became his most well known work.

Temple Thurston was a man of many interests that included golf, tennis, fishing, sketching and painting, and in 1930 an exhibition of his watercolours was held in a London gallery. Following a game of golf during the winter of 1933, he contracted influenza which developed into pneumonia and he died in London on 19 March; he was 53.

Compiled from the following sources:
The Times Monday March 20 1933
The Princess Grace Irish Library of Monaco

AUTHOR'S NOTE
and
ACKNOWLEDGEMENT

I came upon Temple Thurston's book *The 'Flower of Gloster'*[1] at a time when I was working on a history of the Thames locks. It led me to follow his journey of discovery, albeit on foot, and see how much had changed. Temple Thurston's journey was an indulgence and my reconstruction of his journey is also an indulgence. And just as Temple Thurston wrote about certain aspects of his journey that pleased him, while making no mention of others, I have done the same.

When Temple Thurston set out along the Oxford canal in early May 1911, he had no firm idea where his journey would lead him. He left the Oxford canal with Birmingham in mind, but as he entered the industrial Midlands he did not like what he saw and he turned back to the Stratford canal. At Stratford he was faced with a dilemma as there was no towing path alongside the river Avon to assist a horse-drawn boat. At this stage there is little doubt he had the Thames and Severn canal in mind, though to get there he would have to return along the Stratford canal in order to reach Tewkesbury. Instead he walked along country roads and lanes while the *Flower of Gloster* made a circuitous journey, meeting him at Tewkesbury. From there he made his way to the Thames and Severn canal, ending his journey at Inglesham where the canal joined the river Thames.

I should like to express my gratitude to Professor John Barron, former Master of St Peter's College, Oxford, for showing me Canal House and the adjoining garden.

The photographs reproduced in this book were taken over a period of four years (2000-03) with a Leica IIf and 5cm Elmar lens; the film, Ilford Pan F.

John Kemplay
January 2004

1. *The 'Flower of Gloster'* by E Temple Thurston, Williams & Norgate, London 1911. Reprinted by David & Charles, 1968, and by Alan Sutton, 1984.

1

ON DISCOVERY

Ernest Temple Thurston 'believed that the world is a place to wander in.' On a fine morning in early spring his thoughts were to 'sling a knapsack across his shoulders, drop the key of the house in the deepest corner of his pocket, and set out down the road of discovery.' But he was aware that to discover is no longer uppermost in the mind of many of us, and guide-books all too often lessen the freshness of seeing something new. The traveller sees what others have seen before him, and on embarking upon a tour comprising the largest number of sights in the shortest space of time, little of the delights to be seen are registered. With these thoughts in his mind, Temple Thurston decided he would explore some of the canals of England; he would engage a boat and a boatman to take him on a trip of discovery, and though he had no fixed plan in his mind, he went along to the canal basin at Regent's Park to make enquiries. Some of the bargemasters listened to him with amusement and directed him to the offices of the canal company where an official pointed out to him that to hire a canal boat was one thing, but to hire a boatman was quite another: 'you see,' he said, 'they're not gentlemen.' But the official's misgivings did not deter Temple Thurston whose main concern was whether or not it was possible for him to hire a boat. The official consulted some papers and informed him that there was a narrow boat at Oxford that previously had worked the Thames and Severn canal, carrying stone and timber. It had recently undergone a refit at Braunston and the owner most likely would be prepared to hire her out for a month or so; her name was the *Flower of Gloster*. The official advised Temple Thurston to enquire how much it would cost to hire the *Flower of Gloster*, but Temple Thurston knew even before he had seen her that he would take her at any price, and promptly he set out for Oxford.

He had visited Oxford only once before on a New Year's eve when he was taken to Magdalen College for a carol service in Hall, noted for its 'linenfold' panelling and woodcarving of 1541. He was given mulled claret in a silver jug and there were plates of mince-pies. Sometime before midnight the lights were extinguished and by the glow of an open fire the choir sang old English carols. At midnight, windows were thrown open to hear the pealing of bells throughout the town, welcoming the New Year.

The year (1911) that Temple Thurston set out on his journey of discovery was a time when the canal era was almost at an end. The building of many of the canals in England had taken place in the late eighteenth and early nineteenth centuries and they had initially shown a good return for those who had invested their money in the canal companies. Canal boats and barges had offered a means of conveying coal, stone, timber and other merchandise in quantities that road transport of the time could not compete with. Some canals were more successful than others, though eventually the age of steam affected them all to a greater or lesser extent; by the mid-nineteenth century the threat of the railways was very real as merchandise could be moved more quickly and economically that way. The railways were also less prone to bad winter conditions, which often would see canals frozen and locks unworkable, and it was therefore inevitable that the waterways of England which once had flourished would gradually drift into disuse and disrepair. The canals Temple Thurston passed along on his voyage of discovery were among those whose useful life was at an end, and in some ways this benefited his leisurely passage.

2

OXFORD

On his arrival at the Oxford Canal Navigation offices, Temple Thurston was pleasantly surprised by what he found. Although the building was constructed of 'grey' stone, age had toned it to shades that brought colour to his imagination and eye. As he passed through a wooden door in a high stone wall, he came into a garden that was overlooked by the canal company's office windows, and there he found an abundance of flowers, aubrieta, lesser periwinkle, double arabis, iris and tulips, fresh after a recent shower of rain. He enquired of the canal company's official when later they walked round the garden, what was his busiest time of the year. 'Spring' replied the official, as he glanced meaningfully at the rows of young plants in a small greenhouse in the garden.[1]

At the canal wharf, Temple Thurston found the *Flower of Gloster* newly painted in 'vivid reds, glaring yellows, greens and black.' These were the colours used for the exterior of the cabin at the aft of the boat and they were also used for water-cans, buckets and the shallow pails for the horse's feed.

Narrow boat decorations can be traced back to a time when the wives of the boatmen began to take their place at the tiller to form a working pair,

1. Canal House, the canal company's offices, was built in 1828 with a double-pitch roof which was later (1855) removed and a second floor built of stone, though not in keeping with the fine original stonework. The building was acquired by St Peter's College in 1961 and is now the Master's Lodgings. The main door leading directly into Canal House is on Bulwarks Lane and from the tetrastyle portico of the building steps lead down to an enclosed garden, which is on the same level as the lower ground floor and the one-time canal wharf. The door through which Temple Thurston entered the garden is in the wall that runs alongside New Road, and the garden is much as he described it. The greenhouse, though easily visible in a photograph of 1928 has long since been removed.

and it was they who introduced standards of cleanliness and a feminine touch to the living quarters of the boat. Decorations comprised bold designs incorporating diamond, heart and club patterns and the use of strong contrasting colours; floral wreaths and views of romanticised castles were added adornments. Temple Thurston believed that the decorative styles employed by the boat people were of Romany gypsy origin, though more recently the theory has been questioned as Romany paintwork was mainly baroque in character, a style that is not evident in narrow boat decoration.

Joseph Phipkin, the owner of the *Flower of Gloster*, settled with Temple Thurston the business of hiring the boat for a month, and Thurston claimed that had it left only the shirt on his back for the forthcoming journey, he would not grudge the sum that changed hands. And he felt that if accidentally he slightly damaged the boat, the owner would no doubt take a philosophical view of his lack of navigational skills.

The next stage was to find a boatman and he asked Phipkin for his advice, which, he claimed, would be worth more to him 'than half the learning in Oxford.' Phipkin asked him how particular he was, to which Temple Thurston replied that he was concerned that the man should at least be kind to his horse. What Temple Thurston was looking for was a decent man and a horse who would guide him through the locks on his journey of discovery and by good fortune Phipkin knew just the right man, his name was Eynsham Harry. He had no work at the time and he could navigate the canals blindfolded as he had worked them most of his life; he had been born on a boat and no doubt he would die on a boat. Temple Thurston wanted to know a little about Eynsham Harry's origins, but Phipkin could say only that some of the boatmen were in a way different; he had studied them and found them a dark, brown-eyed lot. 'You see', he said, 'they never 'malgamate. They fruitify amongst themselves.' One other matter that interested Temple Thurston was Eynsham Harry's name. He discovered that it was not unusual for a boatman to use his forename prefixed by the name of the village or town he came from, and in Harry's case his origins were the village of Eynsham near the Thames above Oxford. This seemed to satisfy Temple Thurston and together with Joseph Phipkin he made haste to a public-house called The Nag's Head, where he was assured of finding Eynsham Harry.

The Nag's Head was an inn situated in Hythe Bridge Street, barely fifty yards from Worcester Street wharf. The floors were covered in sawdust and the benches, though worn, were well-polished. In the bar was a gathering of boatmen, some playing cards while others stood in groups talking and waiting for their next job; it was a scene that reminded Temple Thurston

Canal House, Oxford, was built in 1828 and used as the canal company's offices. The building was acquired by St Peter's College in 1961. The ground floor, which is entered from Bulwarks Lane is the Master's Lodgings.

The Oxford canal seen from the footbridge that spans the entrance of Isis lock. The lock joins the canal with the Thames and is a short distance from Hythe Bridge.

of a drinking-house on the quay-side in Marseilles. There was a little parlour adjacent to the bar where the landlord brought whisky and water to ease the transaction Temple Thurston hoped to make with Eynsham Harry. Phipkin was there to see fair play and he explained to Eynsham Harry that Temple Thurston had hired the *Flower of Gloster* for a month. The conversation drifted around the issue of whether Eynsham Harry would want the job, and the name of another boatman was mentioned who might do it for near two pounds a week. Temple Thurston asked Eynsham Harry how much he would want: 'Well, sur, I should leave that to you', was Harry's reply. Temple Thurston did not hesitate and he offered thirty shillings a week and payment for food for Harry and his horse. 'I'll take it on,' said Eynsham Harry, 'for a month.'

There was nothing more to do other than provision the boat, obtain some signed passes from the canal office and hitch the horse to the tow-rope. And so it was at 4.15 pm on a day early in May that Temple Thurston, seated at the tiller of the *Flower of Gloster*, watched the tow-rope tauten and the boat slowly move away from the wharf. Twenty yards or so ahead on the towing path was Eynsham Harry and his horse, Fanny, who was beginning to get into her stride on the first part of their journey along the Oxford canal.

Over the years much has changed since Temple Thurston left New Road wharf, where the canal company's office was situated. The Nag's Head on the south side of Hythe Bridge Street is now Antiquity Hall, the name given to it when Morrells, the Oxford brewers, sold the building to a new owner. Today the canal is blocked just before Hythe Bridge, and what was Worcester Street wharf is a car park, but the wharf adjacent to New Road has aspired to better things. By the mid nineteen-thirties the canal company had become aware of the increasing value of its land and they sold New Road wharf to William Morris (later Lord Nuffield) who had in mind a site for a new college, even though it was not until April 1949 that the foundation stone of Nuffield College was laid on the site of the wharf.[1]

---

1. The building of Nuffield College in traditional Oxford style was completed in 1958. In that year it became a self-governing college for post-graduate students.

3

THE OXFORD CANAL

The Oxford canal was first proposed in 1768 by Sir Roger Newdigate a Member of Parliament who lived near Coventry and owned a number of coal mines. He saw the potential rewards of shipping coal to Banbury and Oxford and other places along the proposed route of the canal, which he had asked James Brindley to survey and produce plans. But as with all such schemes there were obstacles and these were mainly landowners who were not enamoured of the canal passing through their lands. All this did not deter Sir Roger from pursuing his plans and by 1769 certain of the landed gentry were more disposed to his proposals. There was however opposition from the Chamber of London who saw the movement of coal from the Midlands to Oxford and then on to the Thames and London, as being in conflict with coal from Newcastle-upon-Tyne which was shipped down the east coast in colliers to the London docks and then by Thames barges to Oxford. Hence, a clause was introduced into the Bill prohibiting coal being conveyed from the canal to the Thames at Oxford. There were other cries of opposition to Sir Roger's proposals, though these were put in perspective by an emotive letter written in February 1769 by an unnamed hand. The writer of the letter pointed out that opposition to the canal did not begin to equate with the benefits coal would bring to the poor inhabitants of places along the route of the canal, where coal could not be had at any price.

The subsequent passage of Sir Roger's Bill through the House of Commons was somewhat turbulent, but the Bill received Royal Assent in April 1769 and the Act stated that the canal would pass on its way from near Coventry to Oxford the towns and villages of Brinklow, Newbold, Hillmorton, Braunston, Napton, Wormleighton, Cropredy, Banbury, King's Sutton, Somerton, Heyford, Shipton, Thrupp and Wolvercote.

James Brindley was appointed engineer and surveyor and cutting the canal started in the autumn of 1769 with an agreement that the junction with the Coventry canal would be at Longford, but as this meant the Coventry and Oxford canals would run in parallel for one mile, the junction was instead made at Hawkesbury. At the end of 1769 an important decision was made when all the canal companies in the Midlands decided to set a standard size for their locks so that boats of 74ft 9in by 7ft with a draft of 4ft 4in could pass through them. This determined the size of lock on the Oxford canal at 80ft between heel posts and seven and a quarter feet in width, with a single top gate and two bottom gates.

During the following five years, 40 miles of the canal were cut and trade commenced as far as Napton. Coal transported from the Hawkesbury pits to Napton was then moved by road to Banbury, Bicester, Woodstock and Oxford, and a local Oxford paper commented that the Midlands coal made 'an exceedingly cheerful fire.'

There were of course the usual money problems that arise with schemes of this nature. During the cutting of the canal it had been necessary to build an aqueduct at Brinklow and a short tunnel at Newbold. Later, a longer tunnel was built at Fenny Compton and to assist boatmen through the tunnel, iron rings at 12ft intervals were attached to both walls, which enabled the men to pull their boat through the tunnel instead of the more traditional method of 'legging' that over a period of time caused wear to the lining of a tunnel. With time the Fenny Compton tunnel became a source of unacceptable delays and by 1870 it had been opened up throughout its entire length.

During the early years of construction of the canal, James Brindley died (he was 56), his life having been shortened by 'irregular living, exposure to all weathers, long fasting, and then, heavy feeding when the nervous system was exhausted,' and that was the opinion of his biographer, Samuel Smiles. Brindley's assistant Samuel Simcock took over the programme of construction and on 30 March 1778 the first consignment of 200 tons of coal reached the wharf at Banbury amid a day of festivities. As far as Banbury the line of the canal adhered to Brindley's plans and followed the contours of the hills and valleys, though this did create a particularly tortuous section between Napton and Fenny Compton.

Although the canal company retained its powers to continue the construction of the canal to Oxford, they had raised as much money as the early Act had allowed, and they now had to find the necessary funding to complete the project. At that time the company's financial position was so dire that the Duke of Marlborough, who was a prominent shareholder, paid the outstanding interest that was owed to the company's creditors. From then onwards the years drifted past as surveys were carried out and landowners whose land the canal would pass through were approached so that the value of their land could be assessed.

By 1787 work on the final stage of the canal was under way and plans were prepared for a wharf between Hythe Bridge Street and Worcester Street in Oxford. On New Year's day 1790, and with great rejoicing by the people of the City of Oxford and the ringing of St Thomas's church bells, boats came to the new wharf laden with coal, corn and other merchandise.

During the first decade of the twentieth century a growing trade in cement produced by the Oxford Cement Company's works near Kirtlington, brought extra trade to the canal, which like other canals in England had earlier suffered from competition generated by the railways. As there was no access to the cement works by rail or road, essential materials needed for the making of cement came by canal from the Midlands, though part of the output went no further than Enslow wharf, a short distance south of the works. A few years later the First World War brought about a decline in trade on the canal owing to a loss of manpower, and by 1919 the tonnage of goods transported had fallen considerably. In the intervening years leading to the Second World War, trade failed to recover significantly and it was not until 1942 that there was a resurgence of activity, though mainly on the northern section of the canal. At the same time the Government saw fit to carry out necessary restoration work on the southern section because of the links the canal had with the Grand Union canal at Braunston and the Thames at Oxford, which would add to its use in the event of the route of the Grand Union to London being severed through hostilities. After the war, trade to and from Oxford declined and by the mid 1950s it was almost extinct. But with the decline in trade there was an increase in pleasure traffic, and wharfs which were once used for coal, changed their use to the hire of pleasure craft, thus establishing a new lease of life for the canal.

4

OXFORD TO BANBURY

The canal leading out of Oxford offers little scenery and it was not until they had passed Wolvercote that Temple Thurston began to see the end of what he called 'damned red brick villas.' He was convinced that the houses were the product of jerry-builders, 'men of execrable taste, whose only thought is to build for the profit it will bring them in a life-time'. He had once visited the house of a jerry-builder in a London suburb, to find in the drawing-room bright and bilious yellow papered walls, chairs upholstered in rich maroon and a green cloth upon one table while on another a palm in a pot, and on the walls, photographs of the jerry-builder and his wife.

'Is the canal like this all the way?', Temple Thurston called to Eynsham Harry, fearful that this may be the case. Eynsham Harry's answer was reassuring: 'Oh no, sur, look you, there's fine country soon as you come past Thrupp.'

Thrupp continues to offer today's traveller an element of calm, even though it is but seven miles by canal from the centre of Oxford. As the canal approaches Thrupp it passes under a bridge and enters a straight stretch leading to one of the drawbridges that are a feature of the Oxford canal. Before the drawbridge is The Boat Inn and opposite the inn a Baptist chapel of 1876; and adjoining the inn and running parallel with the canal a terrace of cottages. As the name of the inn implies, this was a meeting place for the boatpeople who worked the canal for a living, and inside the inn are relics of that time: in the bar-room is a copy of the by-laws of the Oxford Canal Navigation, dated 1808; nearby a plan of the navigable canal from near the City of Coventry to the City of Oxford, and in another room a plan of an Oxford canal drawbridge dated 1861. While the bar area of the inn may be little changed, the clientele is quite different;

no longer the working-class boatpeople, but a new breed of boating enthusiasts together with more smartly dressed business people clutching their mobile phones.

Past the drawbridge the canal enters a basin and at the same time takes a sharp left turn to Shipton-on-Cherwell, barely half a mile away. It was at Shipton that Eynsham Harry intended that they should stop for the night and while Harry took Fanny the horse into the village to find stabling, Temple Thurston remained on the boat watching low-flying swallows feed from the surface of the water. It was the first evening of his journey, it had been a hot day and the memory of that peaceful interlude would remain with him for many years.

The dominant feature of Shipton is Holy Cross church with its Norman tower and avenue of trees leading to the porch; the graveyard slopes down to the canal's edge, though the fine elm trees that partly overshadowed the church many years ago are no more. And were Temple Thurston to have known of their eventual loss, he would have been greatly saddened, as there was no place on earth that he would have wished to be buried when the time came, other than beneath the shadow of the elms in Shipton churchyard. Above the churchyard stands Shipton House which at one time had its own entrance to the church through the wall that divides the garden of the house from the churchyard. This short cut for the privileged residents of the house was sealed-up many years ago and only the outline of the gateway, and the steps remain. Though the canal passes between the village and the river Cherwell, it is after Shipton that the canal and river move towards each other and join at Shipton Weir lock, where navigation is on the Cherwell itself until the next lock upstream. Thereafter river and canal stay close through the Cherwell valley as far as Cropredy, where the river veers to the east while the canal continues in its northerly direction. But the peace that Temple Thurston found so long ago at Shipton is no more, for now there is the continual drone of light aircraft that use Oxford airport at Kidlington, a reminder that progress brings with it problems that are often insoluble.

The following day the *Flower of Gloster* made its way past meadows, watched by cattle at the water's edge. From time to time a boat would pass in the opposite direction as well as a fly-boat that had left Birmingham the previous night. Eynsham Harry had planned to be at Somerton in time for lunch and they passed through the Heyfords without stopping. The section of the canal between Lower and Upper Heyford is pleasantly scenic and had Temple Thurston more time at his disposal he would not have been disappointed had he stopped at Lower Heyford. The village takes its name from a ford that crossed the river Cherwell and was used each year for the hay harvest. The church of St Mary borders the canal and is but a short distance from the village square, which has the Bell Inn on one side and near the centre of the square there is a fine old tree. At the time Temple Thurston and Eynsham Harry passed through Lower Heyford it would have been unthinkable that the peace of this part of the Cherwell valley would eventually be disrupted. In 1914 a local farmer sold his two farms with 160 acres of adjoining land to the Ministry of Defence and in the following year wooden hangers appeared on the land and an airfield began to take shape for training pilots. It closed at the end of the First World War only to be re-commissioned in 1928 to train pilots to fly different types of bomber aircraft. In 1939 Upper Heyford airfield became part of RAF Bomber Command and continued to be used for training aircrews. At that time the levels of noise would hardly be a matter for complaint by the people of Heyford as the seriousness of Britain's position at the beginning of the Second World War would not have been lost on them. But worse was to come when in 1950 the United States Air Force established a presence at Upper Heyford, which was to last for more than forty years. But these events were ahead of the time the *Flower of Gloster* was making its leisurely progress towards Somerton.

In his survey of the final line of the canal, Robert Whitworth decided that the canal should not cross the river Cherwell twice between Upper Heyford and Somerton, as this would have required two aqueducts. Instead he used about a mile of the Cherwell for the canal and dug a new channel for the river. When this change was made in 1790, legal proceedings were instigated against the contractors cutting the canal, but the Oxford Canal Navigation Company successfully defended the action and the change in the course of the Cherwell remains to this day.

At Somerton they stopped at a 'little inn by the canal-side'[1] and while the publican's wife was preparing lunch, Temple Thurston took Eynsham Harry with him to see St James's church whose most striking exterior feature is the fifteenth century battlemented parapet round the nave, aisles and tower. When he discovered where to find the key he was surprised that a boy was deputed to carry it and at the same time accompany Eynsham Harry and himself during the visit. Perhaps Temple Thurston felt that he and Eynsham Harry presented an odd couple; Harry with rough jacket and

---

1.   There has never been a canal-side inn at Somerton. Temple Thurston meant the Railway Inn, which is on the road leading into the village and about 50yd from the canal. The inn went out of business in the 1960s and the building is now a private residence.

trousers and shirt open at the neck, Temple Thurston wearing a coloured tie, a gold watch chain and a crease in his trousers. The boy explained that two weeks earlier visitors to the church had stolen from the altar an old silver chalice, and even though there was nothing else in the church worth stealing, he had to accompany visitors.[1] Temple Thurston told Eynsham Harry how the church had been built 900 years ago (in fact it is mainly fourteenth century). 'Well,' said Eynsham Harry after a pause, 'I 'old wi' churches in their proper place.' Temple Thurston pondered for a moment, but declined to press Harry for the meaning of his profound statement.

From Somerton they made their leisurely way to Banbury, better known for its cross and nursery rhyme than its position at that time as the principal market town of Oxfordshire. The original medieval cross had been destroyed by Puritans in 1602, while the present cross of 1859, which commemorates the marriage of Victoria, Princess Royal, with the Crown Prince of Prussia, is believed to occupy a site different from that of the original cross. Temple Thurston's view of the history of the original cross was that only a fine line separated the end of vandalism and the beginning of religious zeal. Not surprisingly he found himself greatly disappointed by the present cross as well as the town itself, but he admitted that the Reindeer Inn still retained its beauties, although the Globe Room was dismantled in the year of his visit and the ceiling, oak panelling and stone mullion window were bought by a London firm. In 1964 the panelling was found in a London store and acquired by the Banbury Borough Council who in 1981 returned it to the Reindeer Inn. During his wanderings about the town, Temple Thurston noted particularly the many agricultural machines on show and they reminded him of his meeting a farmer in the south of Ireland who had hired a reaper and binder to harvest the wheat in his fields. As they watched the machine cut and bind the wheat into sheaves, the farmer turned to him and said: 'Shure, 'tis the divil in ut! . . .' He could understand the way it reaped, but how it knotted the twine as it bound the sheaves was beyond him.

1. St James's church is still in possession of an old silver chalice, though it is no longer kept in the church.

5

BANBURY TO WARWICK

After leaving Banbury, Temple Thurston realised that until now he had not grasped the full meaning of travelling. He felt that the insensate desire of the traveller to get to his destination as quickly as possible was to 'crush Time beneath his heel.' If a man must travel from Oxford to Birmingham in a few hours then at least once in his life he should take a boat from Oxford and do it in five days. Eynsham Harry's oblique comment on the subject left Temple Thurston short of words: 'Well, sur, men have peculious ideas of how they shall enjoy themselves, and they most ways signifies what sort of men they are . . . I had a week in London once, and there was a friend of mine what spent every evening going to the theatre. I've never thought properly of him since.'

The *Flower of Gloster* continued to make its way in leisurely fashion with Fanny the horse ambling quietly along the towing path, just keeping the rope from sagging in the water. It was a time for conversation as Temple Thurston and Eynsham Harry were together in the aft part of the boat with Harry at the tiller. Temple Thurston asked him how he found enjoyment in life and was surprised when he learned that Eynsham Harry's occupation in his spare time was birds-nesting. When Eynsham Harry was a boy he saw no point in birds-nesting unless he took the eggs, but as he gained maturity he found enjoyment in simply discovering nests and looking, but not taking. He allowed his son to take only one egg from a nest for his collection, but if he, Eynsham Harry, found a nest, he would not tell of its whereabouts. It was from that moment to the end of the journey that Temple Thurston knew he would never regret the thirty shillings a week that had been the agreement he made with Eynsham Harry in the parlour of the Nag's Head in Oxford. Had it been only this one characteristic of Eynsham Harry's life he had learned, the thirty shillings were worth it. As their conversation drifted on, Fanny would cast a wistful glance at the young, green hawthorn shoots by the side of the towing path, and as she stepped closer to them, Eynsham Harry would crack his whip and she would let her ears droop, knowing that she had been found out.

At this stage of their conversation the red-tiled roofs of the village of Cropredy came into view and Eynsham Harry called a halt. When passing through Cropredy he would always go to the Red Lion for a drink.

On entering Cropredy there is a wharf on the left and passing under the first road bridge there is on the left a private house and garden that was once a toll house and coal wharf. Adjacent to the house the canal narrows where boats were gauged to determine the load they were carrying. Almost immediately after is Cropredy bridge and lock and along the narrow road that leads from the bridge is a terrace of houses and the Red Lion. Opposite on raised ground is the church. Like many country inns of the time, Temple Thurston found sawdust on the floors, while sunlight passing through the lead-lighted windows created patterns of gold. In the middle of the morning he found the parlour empty, though later some farm-hands arrived and he and Eynsham Harry played a game with them using a board marked out as a sundial, with each division bearing a number. As the game progressed, Temple Thurston made a mental comparison between the atmosphere he found at the Red Lion and what he would have found on entering a London club; although he would be known, he doubted whether he would have received such a friendly welcome as at the Red Lion.

There had been less peaceful times in the history of Cropredy; in the autumn of 1642, the time of the first major battle of the English Civil Wars at Edgehill, Cropredy saw units of the King's army dispersed in the nearby fields. It was a time when the royalist and parliamentarian armies did not know where the other was, and by accident had run into each other at Wormleighton. And though the following battle of Edgehill was inconclusive, King Charles may have claimed victory had he been better served by his supporters who had misused their infantry at a critical time of the engagement.

It was little more than an hour after the *Flower of Gloster* had left Cropredy that Eynsham Harry and Fanny came to a halt on the towing path and Harry called to Temple Thurston. 'Look you, sur, that bridge . . . 'tis called old town bridge.' Eynsham Harry said he did not know the name of the extinct town, but he had heard that pots and the like had been dug up in the nearby fields. Now, the fields were full of larks' nests, and this was a signal to tie up Fanny and the *Flower of Gloster* and wander through the fields to the village of Wormleighton with its crown of trees looking out to the surrounding countryside.

14

The Red Lion at Cropredy is probably little changed from the time of Temple Thurston's visit in 1911. It overlooks the graveyard of the church of St Mary which is raised above road level.

Cropredy lock. The house on the left was most likely accommodation for a lock-keeper or lengthman when the canal was used by commercial traffic.

No doubt Eynsham Harry was referring to bridge 133, as it is from there that a footpath leads to St Peter's church and to the south of the footpath is the site of a mediaeval village on sloping ground between Wormleighton and the canal. This had once been the community that Eynsham Harry knew as 'old town'. It comprised a large field with irregular boundaries which was characteristic of late mediaeval and Tudor enclosures used for sheep farming; though an unusual feature was the double banks and ditches, many set with trees, forming the boundaries.

When they reached Wormleighton, Temple Thurston felt that it was a corner of the world in which he could wish gently to pass the rest of his life. The church of St Peter is built of Hornton stone and is mostly thirteenth century, while the remains of the manor house, built by John Spencer between 1516 and 1519 following his purchase of Wormleighton from William Cope for £1900, may once have been as grand as Compton Wynyates. What remains of the manor house was visited by Temple Thurston who was taken round by a maid and shown a room panelled in 'warm brown oak'. Here he found an old lady seated by a window with her sewing basket and in her hands a piece of embroidery. He felt his intrusion into the room unjustified and he gracefully bowed his way out.

Detached from all that remains of the house is a large round-arched gatehouse built (1613) of brown Marlstone quarried from the escarpment at nearby Stoneton. The estate housing is also of stone, built in the Tudor-style and gabled, and as a whole, the village is very much as it was when it was built, though, as then, the village is still without a public house.

From Wormleighton the path of the canal becomes tortuous as it follows the 400ft contour of the land. It is also the summit level of the canal, forming an eleven mile stretch from Claydon to Marston Doles. As the *Flower of Gloster* approached Napton and the junction with the Warwick and Napton canal, Temple Thurston suggested that they take it and make for Warwick for the night. But before Warwick, the canal passes through the Old Town of Leamington Spa and it may have been that the passage of the *Flower of Gloster* as it passed Clemens Street and made its way alongside the Old Warwick Road, showed Temple Thurston the drab part of what was once a fashionable spa town. Had they stopped, it is but a short distance to the attractive Jephson Gardens (which has recently undergone a pleasing transformation) and the Parade with its then fashionable shops. It was in 1838 that Queen Victoria bestowed the title 'Royal' upon Leamington and it was during her reign that it achieved the height of its popularity as a spa town. Although no longer fashionable, its architecture comprising Georgian, Regency and early-Victorian houses and buildings is a considerable attraction.

On their arrival at Warwick, Temple Thurston walked into the town and noted particularly the countless volumes about Warwick in the booksellers' windows, and this reminded him that the voyage he and the *Flower of Gloster* were taking was one of discovery. There was nothing in Warwick that had not been discovered already and he decided not to write one word of its history; and neither shall I.

The Gatehouse at Wormleighton was built in 1613 of brown Marlstone and presents a round archway surrounded by armorial devices. It replaced an earlier and even grander gatehouse.

Central Hospital, Hatton, was the Warwickshire county asylum. The first patients were admitted in 1852 although it was not until 1933 that voluntary admission was permitted. The few remaining patients were transferred in 1995 to St Michael's Hospital, Warwick, and Central Hospital was sold to developers for housing.

6

WARWICK TO STRATFORD

The industrial midlands, or the Black Country as Temple Thurston preferred to call it, was not new to him; he had driven along many of the roads that made up what he described as 'an awful yet wonderful part of the world.' Perhaps he indulged in writers' license when he wrote about 'The black sweeping hills with scrubby bushes leafless and dead; the men and women, white-faced and dirty with the everlasting falling of the sooty air;' but for all that, he acknowledged the greatness of the industrial lands.

From Warwick the canal makes its way to Birmingham and Temple Thurston thought, even though he scarcely understood why, he was following a route that was hardly one of discovery, and yet he felt he must go on. And he ignored Eynsham Harry's warning: 'If it's the country you want to see, sur, then have my advice and do nothing wi' Birningame.' After a few miles they reached the Hatton flight of locks which lift the canal 144ft. The locks were seven feet wide and would accommodate only one narrow boat at a time, but later, in 1932, wider locks were built alongside the narrow locks. This extra flight was added because the canal had continued to suffer from competition from the railways and it was thought that by increasing the capacity of the Hatton flight, traffic would move more easily and hence the transportation of merchandise would be quicker and trade improved.

At the time the *Flower of Gloster* passed through the Hatton flight, Temple Thurston found little to please him, even though the flight was not without interest. As they progressed through the locks they passed Asylum Wharf, though Temple Thurston was unaware of its significance as no doubt Eynsham Harry felt it prudent not to mention the asylum, being well aware that Temple Thurston had only an eye for the delights of the countryside.

Less than half a mile from the wharf stood the Warwickshire county lunatic asylum. When an Act (Victoria) of 1845 compelled counties to finance the building of asylums, John Conolly, then medical superintendent of the Middlesex asylum at Hanwell, advised the county of Warwickshire to build their asylum at Hatton. Perhaps it was planned or it may have been fortuitous that the site selected was adjacent to the Hatton flight of locks, and the wharf just above bridge 53 became the landing stage for the building materials used in the construction of the asylum. It was opened in 1852 and comprised an elegant main building with an imposing clock tower and a secondary building called the Idiot Asylum. Within the grounds, Hill Farm provided produce, while coal was brought down from Birmingham each week by two narrow boats and moved from the wharf in barrows manned by the inmates. Later, in 1895, a house (Edgehill) was built for the medical superintendent, and thereafter progress in mental health continued for 100 years when the land and buildings were sold to developers in 1995. Although new houses have been built in the grounds, the original asylum buildings have been kept and converted into modern apartments.

There is a long pound between Hatton top lock and the flight of five locks at Knowle, and when the *Flower of Gloster* had passed through, Temple Thurston knew he had been wrong to continue his journey to Birmingham. But he stuck to his pride and he and Eynsham Harry continued on their way, though Eynsham Harry was biding his time to remind Temple Thurston of the warning he had given him. It was before they reached Solihull that Temple Thurston realised the fields and trees were less, and ugly buildings had begun to line the canal-side, and not least, Eynsham Harry's prediction of finding dead cats and dogs floating in the water had become a reality.

Temple Thurston knew that to persevere further would be pointless and he asked Eynsham Harry what they should do. Harry had his answer ready, they should return to Kingswood where there is a junction with the Stratford-upon-Avon canal and there Temple Thurston would find the tranquillity he sought in the fine Warwickshire countryside.

THE STRATFORD-UPON-AVON CANAL

The Stratford canal was intended as a link between the town of Stratford and the coal mines and factories of the Midlands, a link that would bring coal to Warwickshire villages and in return a trade in corn. Josiah Clowes was appointed engineer for the project as he was a very experienced canal builder and had been principal assistant to Robert Whitworth during the building of the Thames and Severn canal. The line of the Stratford canal, as proposed by John Snape of Birmingham, was from King's Norton on the Worcester and Birmingham canal to Stratford, the route passing through Lapworth and forming a junction with the Warwick and Birmingham canal at Kingswood. It was planned that the canal would end near the site of the present railway station at Stratford instead of joining the river Avon. This was because of opposition from the Worcester and Birmingham Canal Company who were concerned that a junction with the Avon would bring about a loss of trade on their canal, as traffic on the proposed Stratford canal would be able to pass by way of the Avon through Evesham and Tewkesbury to the river Severn below Worcester.

After much negotiation among the interested parties, work began in November 1793 at King's Norton on the northern end of the canal and by 1796 construction work had been completed to Hockley Heath, though at that stage all the funding for the work had been used and there was no more money to proceed further. In the years that followed it is very likely that the efforts of William James, a land-agent, managed to get the construction of the canal on the move again and cutting resumed in 1812; a year later the canal opened to Wootton Wawen, thereby bringing trade in coal by road to Alcester. In 1813, William James bought the upper Avon navigation and no doubt he had in mind joining the Stratford canal with the Avon in order to create a through route to the river Severn, and hence compete with trade on the Worcester and Birmingham canal.

The change in the line of the Stratford canal so that it could join the Avon at The Bancroft, was inevitable, even though the Worcester and Birmingham Canal Company had strongly opposed the scheme. An Act (George III) of 1815 enabled the necessary work to proceed and the canal was completed in June 1816 when it was declared that the conveyancing of coal, iron, corn and other articles of merchandise could now begin between Stratford and Birmingham; and this led to the best Wednesbury and Tipton coal being available at the Avon warehouse for 10d a hundredweight. Although trading on the canal reached a peak in 1838, the growing competition from the railways resulted in the canal being bought by the Great Western Railway Company in 1846 and thereafter trade declined. But all this happened long before the *Flower of Gloster* made its way down the 13 mile stretch of canal between Kingswood Junction and Stratford.

In some respects the Stratford canal was fortunate it was taken over by the Great Western Railway in the mid-nineteenth century. Whereas some canals had fallen into the hands of the receivers and rapidly deteriorated, the railway company let the Stratford canal fall gently into disuse as traffic was gradually transferred to the railway. And though the process of disuse was slow, it was not until the end of the Second World War when the canal was transferred to the British Transport Commission that the southern section between Kingswood Junction and Stratford ceased to be navigable. The situation in 1958 seemed dire when the Warwickshire County Council proposed the abandonment of the canal under an Act (Victoria) of 1888, but through the efforts of the Inland Waterways Association the southern section of the canal was transferred to the National Trust on a five year lease and during this period the canal was restored to navigational use. It was officially re-opened in July 1964 and the Trust exercised its option to acquire the freehold of the waterway.

*

Temple Thurston did not for one moment regret having taken Eynsham Harry's advice to return to Kingswood Junction and join the Stratford canal. After the dullness of the Birmingham canal he once more found meadows and white thorn hedges half in bloom, and again in the hedgerows he occasionally saw a crab-apple tree, its blooms pink-white. By the water's edge grew reeds, for in the year of his journey of discovery very little traffic passed along the canal to Stratford and the luxuriant growth of weeds in the crevices of the lock gates testified to the little they were used.

As Temple Thurston lay stretched out on the cabin roof of the *Flower of Gloster* absorbing the May sunshine, he wondered how man could care for the march of progress that eventually would destroy the tranquillity of his passage. He was well aware of the effect the railways had made upon the canal system, and he may well have seen how the development of the motor vehicle would open up transportation of goods by road. But he did not know then that the stillness of his passage through the locks carrying the canal down from Kingswood Junction to the village of Lowsonford, would in time be disturbed by the continuous noise of traffic on a nearby motorway. Fortunately for Temple Thurston, he arrived at Lowsonford unaffected by the march of progress that so concerned him.

The canal passes through the centre of the village (known in the early 1800s as Lonesome Ford) and at the lock-side, just before the road bridge, is one of the barrel-vaulted lock-keeper's cottages that are so distinctive and unique to the Stratford canal. Temple Thurston found the village more peaceful than any he had encountered on his journey, and it seemed to him that all men and things were asleep, even though he saw farm labourers entering and leaving the White Horse Inn, so there was work to be done

Lock Cottage, Lowsonford, is the only barrel-vaulted lock-keeper's cottage on the
Stratford canal that is still in its original state; it is administered by the Landmark
Trust. It has been suggested that the unique shape of these cottages is a result of
the re-use of timber arching made as supports during the building of bridges on the
canal.

Yarningale Farm appears to be little changed since the time of Temple Thurston's visit, though the orchard he described is no longer in evidence.

somewhere. He felt that one could spend a summer in the village and forget there existed a world outside, and as the *Flower of Gloster* passed through the lock, children appeared and watched from the low wall of the bridge, for then it was something of an event for a boat to pass through the village. Even the lock-keeper's dog, sunning itself on the lock-side, roused itself to watch the passage of the *Flower of Gloster*. But looking back to earlier years, when the Stratford canal was a busy waterway, the boatmen passing through may well have been an intrusion to the way of village life.

Today the village of Lowsonford retains a certain charm and peaceful disposition. The canal passes by the back of the Fleur de Lys, which is the only inn and is made up of three interconnecting buildings, though at the time of the passage of the *Flower of Gloster* the buildings were used differently. At the north end was a blacksmith's shop, while the centre building was the inn which comprised a 'tap room' and 'smoke room'. The south end of the buildings was living accommodation for the landlord, though the back section was kept as a separate cottage. It is fortunate, as in other canal-side inns, that there are photographs showing how parts of the village once looked in the late nineteenth century. One shows the ford and another the White Horse Inn, and of course the Fleur de Lys. In these photographs can be imagined the peace that Temple Thurston found, for at the time of his journey the village was in between a changing pattern of transport. Working boats on the canal had dwindled away and would entirely leave the southern part of the canal by the nineteen-twenties; the railway branch line to Henley-in-Arden which passed through the north end of the village had fallen out of use when a direct line was built between Henley and Birmingham; and the motor vehicle was yet to make an impact on the life of the village. Indeed, Temple Thurston was fortunate with his timing.

Although over the years the two inns have changed, the White Horse Inn now being a private residence, there is one building that has remained as it was; it is the barrel-vaulted lock-keeper's cottage that has retained its original features since the time it was built about 1810. When the National Trust acquired the canal they found that the tenant of the lock cottage had lived there all his life. Ned Taylor was born in 1921, his father was a farm labourer and it is likely that he and his wife rented the cottage from the Great Western Railway, who then owned the canal. As it was a controlled tenancy, the National Trust decided to renovate the cottage, maintaining its original features. They then passed the administration of the cottage to the Landmark Trust. It is therefore Ned's cottage as it is known locally, that is the remaining example of the barrel-vaulted cottages on the Stratford canal in its original state. Others have passed into private hands and this has led to alterations and extensions which have damaged the unique design of these cottages.

From Lowsonford the *Flower of Gloster* passed through pleasant countryside. But as they reached Yarningale aqueduct, which carries the canal over a stream that leads to the river Alne, Eynsham Harry realised they had forgotten to buy milk. Rather than return to the village, Temple Thurston decided to walk to what he thought was a farmhouse on the crest of a hill. The steep grass slope leading to the farmhouse had been made into an orchard and the rows of apple trees were in blossom offering a sight as fine as any he had seen. He found the farmhouse with a yard where chickens scratched amongst some hay and a cow watched him from the edge of the orchard. Except for a black cat, the house seemed deserted and his knocking on the door brought no response. As the door was unlocked he entered and found on an old Victorian horse-hair sofa a very old lady fast asleep. In the hope of finding the farmer's wife he walked through to the kitchen and though there was no one, he found five cans of milk on a slab of slate. Filling the jug he had brought with him, he left a note with some money and departed with haste – the old lady slept on.[1]

As they continued on their way to Preston Bagot it may not have crossed Temple Thurston's mind that the accommodation bridges on the canal were of an unusual design. At the time the canal was constructed it bisected tracts of farmland and accommodation bridges were built so that farmers could move their cattle and farm implements from one piece of land to another. These bridges were not built to the same structural requirements as a road bridge, which would take the towing path beneath it. On the Stratford canal the waterway narrows as it passes under the accommodation bridges which comprise a brick pier on either side of the water supporting iron sections in the form of cantilevers that do not quite meet in the centre. This was to enable the boatman to pass the tow-rope through the gap and so remove the delays that would be caused by undoing the rope from the horse.

Preston Bagot is fortunate in one respect as the line of the canal is a comfortable distance from the centre of the village. And though the village is a walk away from Preston Bagot lock, it has sufficient charm together

1. Yarningale Farm is an old timber framed house about 50yd from Yarningale lock and beside what is now a public footpath. The house appears to be little changed since the time Temple Thurston visited it, though the orchard has gone.

The Stratford canal between Lowsonford and Preston Bagot is probably the most scenic section of the canal.

Canal-side woodland at Preston Bagot.

with the splendidly situated church on high ground to make the detour worth while; but Temple Thurston had decided to stay on course to Wootten Wawen and Stratford.

Between Preston Bagot and Wilmcote there is only one lock and the *Flower of Gloster* would have made good progress, though it would appear that Temple Thurston was not sufficiently steeped in the works of William Shakespeare to want to walk into the village of Wilmcote to see Mary Arden's house which is a farmhouse named after Shakespeare's mother and believed to have been her home before she married and moved to Stratford. At Wilmcote there is a flight of locks of which five have a side pond to maintain a sufficient level of water as boats lock up or down the flight; but Temple Thurston showed no interest in such matters. As the canal drops down on its way to Stratford the passage of the *Flower of Gloster* would have been through agricultural land and unspoiled countryside. Progress, however, was not far away and the gradual sprawl of Stratford accelerated during the latter half of the twentieth century and from lock 51 the canal increasingly is flanked by industrial estates. But were Temple Thurston to enter the canal basin at Stratford today he would find a sight much more in line with his aesthetic leanings. What in fact he did find as he passed under the bridge that leads to the canal basin, was an industrial site comprising a coal wharf and to one side of the basin the marshalling yards of the Stratford and Moreton Railroad. The railroad was in fact a tramway with horse-drawn wagons that passed over a narrow brick-built bridge across the river Avon and on to Moreton-in-Marsh and Shipston-on-Stour. Today the basin is unchanged, though the yards are partly gardens and a public house on the site of what was once Cox's yard. But going back before the time of Temple Thurston's visit there were two canal basins, though owing to a decline in trade on the canal the second basin was filled-in in 1902 and eventually became part of the site for a new theatre that was built in 1932. The gardens either side of the existing basin are known as the Bancroft Gardens and the theatre is of course the Shakespeare Memorial Theatre. The gardens are so named because the site occupied by both canal basins and marshalling yards was once common land known as The Bancroft, and used by the townsfolk as grazing land for their animals.

Temple Thurston retained only one clear memory of Stratford, though not of the town but the river where he saw '. . . a lady dressed in white, seated in a pure-white gondola, propelled on the waters of the Avon by a gondolier all clothed in the same colour of virginal simplicity.' At that time Stratford was not just the birthplace of William Shakespeare, it was a town of minor personalities and perhaps one of the more important was Marie

Corelli, the lady in the gondola. Miss Corelli came to Stratford when she was in her early forties and lived with her companion Miss Bertha Vyver. She was noted for wearing white and other light colours, which were then thought unsuitable for a woman who had passed her fortieth birthday. Her presence in Stratford caused much aggravation among certain of the townspeople, even though she was a generous person who helped the town in certain ways. In the first few years of her arrival in Stratford she acquired a punt which she lavishly decorated on annual regatta days, but at a London exhibition some few years later she saw a gondola and promptly bought it. Her purchase came with a 'real' Italian who spent a month instructing a young local man how to propel it. Stratford had seen nothing like this before, and neither had Temple Thurston.[1]

When Temple Thurston and Eynsham Harry returned to the *Flower of Gloster* with supplies they had bought in the town, Temple Thurston had sudden qualms about going back along the Stratford canal to the junction of the Worcester and Birmingham canal, which eventually would lead him to the Thames and Severn canal by way of the river Severn. He therefore quickly made up his mind to send Eynsham Harry and the *Flower of Gloster* back along the route they had just travelled while he would walk, roughly following the line of the river Avon, which at that time could not be navigated by horse-drawn boats, and he would meet Eynsham Harry at Tewkesbury.

And so they parted company, Eynsham Harry, Fanny the horse and the *Flower of Gloster* returning along the Stratford canal while Temple Thurston, knapsack on his back, set out in a south-westerly direction on his continuing journey of discovery.

1. Marie Corelli was the pseudonym of Mary Mackay (1855-1924). Although she was trained as a pianist, she turned to writing and her first novel was published when she was in her early thirties. Her novels savagely attacked both the established churches and the society of the day and she considered her mission was to assert the underlying spiritual quality of life as it really was. Her output was prolific and she quickly became a best-selling author.
   In her memoir, *Rosemary for Stratford-on-Avon*, Ursula Bloom recalls that the gondolier wore a scarlet sash, though a painting of unknown date of Miss Corelli in her gondola shows the boat in its traditional Venetian colouring.

7

STRATFORD TO TEWKESBURY

Out of Stratford upon Avon, Temple Thurston took the road that leads to Bidford. But the town had little interest for him and he felt that by becoming a haunt of the Birmingham day tripper it had become 'cruelly modernised'. He had little time for day trippers, the way they went about in swarms, eating and drinking on every possible occasion, while the ordinary traveller, and no doubt he had himself in mind, was more contented with the scenery and buildings. Today, Bidford may no longer possess the charm it held for the Birmingham holiday-makers during the early part of the last century, for in those times the fine stretch of water down to Cleeve Mill would be adorned with rowing-boats and steam launches provided by the proprietor of Holland's Pleasure Grounds, while Bidford bridge was a chosen place for smartly dressed men and women whose revelries would accelerate on Saturday nights, leaving the town to recover its normal way of life during the week days.

On leaving Bidford, Temple Thurston came upon a nunnery that he might easily have passed had it not been for a chance meeting with two elderly ladies whom he had asked for directions to Evesham. Salford Hall at Abbots Salford almost took his breath away. The original Salford Hall had been built in the latter part of the fifteenth century and acted as a residence for monks visiting nearby Evesham Abbey. A new wing was added in 1662 when the hall became the residence of Sir John Alderford, but it was later, from 1808 to 1838, that the hall was used as a nunnery and convent school. The nuns who occupied the hall were the survivors of a Benedictine order originating in this country whose property at Cambrai had been confiscated, and for the period of the French revolution they had been imprisoned. Those who were left finally fled back to England at the end of the eighteenth century and took up residence at Salford Hall. Their time there ended in 1838 when they bought Stanbrook Hall in Worcestershire, subsequently demolishing the hall and building Stanbrook Abbey on the site.

From the time the nuns left Salford Hall the building fell gradually into disuse, though at the time Temple Thurston visited the hall in 1911 it was still in a tolerable condition. He found that upon payment of sixpence a girl would guide him through the interior of the building, and he passed from room to room seeing the priest's hole which was in the original part of the hall and the dormitory where the girls once slept. The dormitory was at the top of the more recent part of the building and ran from front to back. It was well lighted by three dormer windows along one side and windows placed in ogee shaped gables at each end. He ended his visit at the chapel which he found disappointing; to him it showed signs of modern catholicism, 'the cheap finery, the gaudy altar cloth, the ill-painted pictures of the journey of the cross around the walls.' As he left and walked back through the gatehouse with its timber framed gable, he felt that he might have carried away a pleasant memory of the place had it not been for that one discordant note. There was however another discordant note he was not aware of, *The Tragic Legend of Salford Hall*, recounted by the Reverend A B Crane who was the priest who officiated at the chapel in the late nineteenth century. This mysterious story of two sisters who entered the convent school in 1815 and what befell them would have appealed to Temple Thurston in his capacity as a writer and dramatist. The tale, though chilling, is of historical interest as it touches on the customs of the hall and the great kindness shown to the girls by the Abbess and the Sisters, even though they were not of the catholic faith.[1]

In 1939, before the outbreak of the Second World War, Tom Rolt and his wife passed through the gatehouse of Salford Hall as they had time on their hands as they waited for their narrow boat, *Cressy*, to be fitted out at Tooley's yard at Banbury.[2] Their knock at the door of the hall was answered by an old lady who looked after the chapel that had so disappointed Temple Thurston, though now it was the only part of the building still in use. They passed through the hall only to find rooms almost bare of furnishings with paper hanging from the walls, and ceilings stained by damp. As they entered the second storey the scene of ruin was even more marked as holes had appeared in the rotting floors and laths protruded through broken plaster. But the priest's hole was still intact, situated in a corner of a room and in the form of a small cupboard lined

1. *The Tragic Legend of Salford Hall* is published by the proprietors of Salford Hall Hotel, Abbots Salford, Warwickshire.
2. L T C Rolt 1910-1974. Author of *Narrow Boat* and founder member of the Inland Waterways Association.
    Tooley's dry dock has been in use since 1790 and is now scheduled an Ancient Monument.

The bridge across the river Avon at Bidford.

Salford Hall at Abbots Salford was a nunnery and convent school during the years 1808-38. When the nuns moved to Stanbrook Hall near Worcester, Salford Hall was left to George Eyston and remained in his family until the Second World War. Thereafter it deteriorated until it was bought by a private company in 1987. Following restoration it was opened as Salford Hall Hotel.

with shelves. The back of the cupboard and its shelves swung inwards and could be bolted on the inside, forming a well disguised hiding place.

Although an attempt was made to put Salford Hall on a commercial footing in the nineteen-sixties, the venture failed and it was not until 1987 that it was acquired by a private company which undertook major restoration work to bring it back to its former glory. It then opened as Salford Hall Hotel. The chapel is now the main restaurant of the hotel and though in its former capacity it was not to Temple Thurston's liking, today he may easily have viewed it differently.

Leaving Abbots Salford, Temple Thurston continued his journey to Evesham where he realised that Eynsham Harry had been right when he said that no horse-drawn barge would be able to navigate that part of the river. The state of the Avon in 1911 was poor, even though the locks between Evesham and Tewkesbury had been repaired at different times over the past thirty years. Later, in the early nineteen-forties, the Avon had finally become un-navigable above Pershore, though the situation was to change in 1950 with the formation of the Lower Avon Navigation Trust who by 1962 had put the river between Evesham and Tewkesbury in good order. At the time the Trust had completed its work, the Upper Avon Navigation Trust was formed in order to make the river navigable between Stratford and Evesham. But Temple Thurston was not concerned about the navigable state of the Avon, it was the countryside the river flowed through that took his attention. And so he made his way through Evesham and on to the village of Fladbury. As he passed through Evesham it would seem that he gave no thought to the remains of the abbey and the parish churches; perhaps his disappointment over the chapel in the old nunnery had for the time being dampened his interest in ecclesiastical matters. This was his misfortune as there is much that is worthy of seeing. It was in the eleventh century that the abbots created a market town outside the abbey and a century later the churches of St Lawrence and All Saints were built, and although both churches have undergone changes since that time, St Lawrence's church, which at one time served the poorer inhabitants of the parish, held to its low-church tradition and its interior is plain. Even so, there is some interesting stained glass and particularly the fine windows executed by Alexander Gibbs on the north and south sides of the chancel in the mid-nineteenth century. When the parishes of St Lawrence and All Saints were united in 1978, the former church was declared redundant and in the following year it was vested in The Churches Conservation Trust. The latter church has been in continuous use since it was built by the abbots, and is more opulent than the church of St Lawrence. All Saints is endowed with many fine windows and particularly the five light window in the north transept. Executed by the Belgian stained glass worker, J B Capronnier in 1882, it shows the kneeling figure of Mary with the face of Maria Epsley in whose memory the window was created.

The original abbey foundered in about the year 960 and was replaced by another of greater proportions which was consecrated in 1054. Although it became one of the great Benedictine abbeys, Henry VIII had other views and during the Reformation the abbey was broken up and used as building material. Today, all that remains intact is the great gateway which formed the entrance to the abbey courtyard, the almonry that once catered for the sick and poor of the town, and the bell tower which has a fine ring of bells and a carillon that plays secular tunes on weekdays and hymn tunes on Sundays.

On reaching Fladbury, Temple Thurston decided to stay the night. The following morning he took the ferry-boat from the village side of the river to Cropthorne Mill, which he found enchanting and he wished he had been born there. As he stood near the lock that adjoins the mill he met an old woman who had been gathering dandelions in a nearby field. They were for making wine she explained, and she went over the recipe with him, saying: 'Twas well called wine, my old man said - he got quite jolly over it one day, he did.' 'And did you scold him for that?' asked Temple Thurston. Well, 'I've never seen him the same like it since', she replied.

Fladbury has expanded greatly since the time Temple Thurston passed through and today it would hardly be recognised by William Sandys who lived there in the early seventeenth century and was the first to make the Avon navigable. In 1636 he constructed locks and weirs between Stratford and Tewkesbury and although he encountered opposition to his plan of work, he finally succeeded in his task three years later. The barges using the river at that time carried a square sail, though they often needed to be hauled by gangs of men who were hampered in their task by the lack of a continuous towing path.

From Fladbury, Temple Thurston gives no indication of his journey to Eckington bridge, which was such a source of delight that he stopped there, for he felt there was no place on earth better suited for contemplation than a bridge spanning a gently flowing river. It was there he thought of the company of Eynsham Harry that he was enjoying so much on his journey, though he would not forget the glorious days he had been walking to Tewkesbury.

With these thoughts in his mind he passed through Eckington village, though he found no beauties to recommend it. On reaching Nafford, he

Cropthorne mill is one of two mills in Fladbury, both of which are private residences. Cropthorne mill is adjacent to Fladbury lock, which is confusing and caused Temple Thurston to misname it.

Fladbury weir stretches between the two mills.

The view from Eckington bridge looking downstream. It is most likely the same
scene Temple Thurston referred to in his book.

Manor Lane, Little Comberton, where at the time of Temple Thurston's visit there was a steam laundry, bakehouse and village shop. It is probable that Thurston stayed at New Manor House (nearby) as it has an open view of Bredon Hill and is the only house that could have been a farmhouse at that time.

stopped for tea at a thatched farm cottage before climbing Bredon Hill. He would liked to have seen the interior of Woollas Hall, situated half way up the hill, but as it was privately owned he had to forgo the pleasure, though his disappointment was soon offset as he reached the summit of the hill and found the view so fine that he felt God was more generous in the pleasures he gave than any man was able to do. 'Which, by the way,' he thought, 'is what one only has the right to expect.'

In choosing the month of May for his voyage of discovery, Temple Thurston could not have failed to appreciate the abundance of apple blossom, particularly as he passed through the Vale of Evesham, and he was overwhelmed as he reached the village of Little Comberton burnished golden in the glow of the evening sun. Here he found a colony of apple orchards; they surrounded every cottage and the trees filled almost every garden. And the cottages themselves, half-timbered, were washed white between the beams, giving the village a spotless appearance. In a way, the little village in the shadow of Bredon Hill was 'immaculate'. Temple Thurston stayed the night in an old farm-house in the centre of the village. The garden was full of colour, though the farmer's wife had planted her tulips in lines so straight that when his eye ran along them as they stood beneath the windows, he could see how uneven were the old walls of the house itself. From the bedroom window he was able to see the moon as it drifted through interrupted cloud that seemed to lay stationary over Bredon Hill. He compared in his mind the stillness of the village with the never ceasing noise of London traffic at night, a sound he had not heard for more than three weeks. He woke early the following morning to find the sun filtering through the window of his room. The sound of a dog as it guided a flock of sheep to pasture, followed by an old shepherd, signalled the awakening of the village.

Leaving Little Comberton to deal with its new day, Temple Thurston made his way to Tewkesbury where he found some of the old mills empty and the wharfs deserted. But there was life in the form of Eynsham Harry, striding along the wharf to meet him, the *Flower of Gloster* moored nearby and Fanny the horse waiting patiently. Together they went into the town for provisions and Temple Thurston found himself delighted by the splendid tower of the abbey and the old buildings and narrow passages that in ways reminded him of Rouen. Much as he would have liked to spend time in the town, his journey of discovery was nearing its end and he had but a few days more at his disposal, and he was anxious to join the Thames and Severn canal and pass through the Golden Valley.

8

TEWKESBURY TO STROUD

Temple Thurston's journey between Tewkesbury and Stroud produced no word of praise or dislike of what he saw; neither was there a mention of the route that he and Eynsham Harry travelled, though there is only one route they could have taken.[1]

At Tewkesbury the river Avon joins the river Severn and downstream at Gloucester docks there is a junction with the Gloucester and Berkeley canal (now the Gloucester and Sharpness canal), which in turn joins the Stroudwater navigation at Saul. Travelling east from the junction at Saul, the Stroudwater navigation rises through ten locks to reach Stroud where a canal basin defines the beginning of the Thames and Severn canal. It was from there that the *Flower of Gloster* started on the final leg of its journey.

It was a journey that took Temple Thurston through some of the most beautiful scenery he could have wished for. The Golden Valley, through which the canal passed to the summit level, was, in May, an unrivalled display of fresh greens on its wooded slopes and an abundance of spring flowers.

1. It is debatable whether Temple Thurston undertook this part of his journey. It is possible that he returned to London from Tewkesbury and then a few days later took the train to Stroud to meet up again with Eynsham Harry.

9

STROUD TO INGLESHAM

THE THAMES AND SEVERN CANAL

By the end of the seventeenth century the rapidly expanding City of London needed more food, coal and manufactured goods; items that already were being transported from Bristol and the West Country by coaster and overland by wagon. It was evident that a canal would provide an easier way to transport these goods than the hazardous sea voyages and laborious land journeys. And it was because of this need for a new route that the Thames and Severn canal became the first trunk waterway to be proposed as a more convenient way to transport goods from the west of England to London.

Although a number of routes the canal might take were considered, it was the Stroud valley that attracted most attention owing to the prosperous woollen industry which supplied manufacturers of cloth whose mills were in the valley. As there were already difficulties in transporting the cloth, it seemed propitious that a canal passing through the valley and giving access to the Severn in one direction and London by way of the Thames in the other direction, would solve these problems. And so in the first instance a navigation called the Stroudwater Canal was cut between Framilode on the Severn and the town of Stroud. It was completed in July 1779 and although the proprietors of the navigation were anxious to promote the next phase of their canal project, it was not until 1781 that they and other interested parties commissioned a survey between Stroud and Cricklade in Wiltshire. The surveyor easily saw the difficulties in trying to join the proposed canal with the Thames at Cricklade because of the restricted width and depth of the river, and he suggested Lechlade, some miles downstream, as a more suitable junction. Hence, the proprietors of the new canal called upon Robert Whitworth, James Brindley's most able assistant, to give them an opinion. His report, completed in December 1782, was based on imprecise information given him and he had to decide for himself that goods transferred from Severn trows to barges and narrow boats should be carried out in the region of Stroud; a decision that determined the size of the locks on the new canal.

The Thames and Severn Canal Act of 1783 (George III) was an Act for making a navigable canal from the river Thames at or near Lechlade to join with the Stroudwater canal at Walbridge, Stroud, with a cut from the said canal near Siddington to the town of Cirencester. The Act received Royal Assent in April of that year and Josiah Clowes was appointed surveyor and engineer to assist Robert Whitworth in setting out the navigation. But Whitworth did not give the construction of the canal as much of his time as the proprietors reasonably expected of him, and it was only the nine mile summit level which includes the Sapperton tunnel that is wholly attributed to him. Work started at Stroud in 1784 and proceeded through the well populated valley where there were mills and the homes of landowners whose gardens and orchards were often breached by the cutting of the canal. As work progressed, locks and bridges were built and the first vessel entered Walbridge Lower lock on 31 January 1785.

It was at this stage that a more taxing part of the construction began, as the Golden Valley above Chalford presented a site less than ideal for a canal owing to the porous nature of the floor of the valley. In fact, it was to become a source of weakness that remained until the end of the useful life of the canal. Owing to the incline of the valley the canal required many locks and their frequency increased in the last half of the assent. Nevertheless, work as far as Daneway bridge was completed in 1786 and below the bridge a basin was constructed with an adjoining coalyard and warehouse. Above the bridge and adjacent to the summit lock a house had been built in 1784, which was used as accommodation for some of the workers and later became a public house called the Bricklayers' Arms. In addition to the canal basin a road was constructed to enable the transportation of coal by waggon to the village of Sapperton and beyond.

Although mistakes were made during the cutting of the canal through the Golden Valley, the work itself was relatively easy. The real test came when work started on the tunnel that would run beneath Sapperton Hill and Hailey Wood and emerge not far from the village of Coates. Robert Whitworth calculated 3850yd as the length of the tunnel and decided that the height and width of the bore should each be fifteen feet. The method of work was to start at each end and sink 22 shafts along a straight line. As it turned out, the final length was 3817yd.

Unhappily, work on the Sapperton tunnel did not proceed as efficiently as it might have done. Charles Jones, who was a stonemason and miner, had been brought to the notice of the committee of the canal company by Josiah Clowes, and although Jones was not the only contender for the contract to do the tunnelling, his bid was sufficiently low to secure him the work at seven guineas a yard. There was, however, another side to Jones the committee had no knowledge. Jones was inept when it came to handling money and he had debts. His workmen were not paid regularly and he had to ask the committee for cash advances to satisfy his creditors. But for all that, work on the tunnel went ahead and after about twelve weeks, Jones and his men reached open rock as they progressed from the Daneway end. This presented certain difficulties and it was the opinion of Josiah Clowes that Jones must increase the height and width of the tunnel wall and line it with masonry. This Jones had to do within the contract price, an undertaking that many years later was looked upon as an unreasonable unpaid addition to his work-load, even though the canal company may well have been within their rights. As time went on, further difficulties were created by Jones whose mens' wages were in arrears and his creditors were closing in on him. Eventually he was arrested for debt and imprisoned, though he managed to extricate himself with only one day in hand before the canal company could dismiss him for being away from the site for 28 days. These upheavals undermined progress on the tunnel and when Jones was again arrested for debt, the canal company gave him three months' notice to complete outstanding work and leave the site. Jones, however, was not prepared to leave without a fight and he, or lawyers acting for him, filed a Bill in Chancery claiming that he had completed the work on the entire length of the tunnel in the four years stated in the contract. In fact he had completed, though not properly finished, a little less than a third of the length of the tunnel, and the canal company made clear that this was a matter they could easily prove, and Jones had no alternative but to drop the proceedings. However, Jones had not been finally dislodged from the site when the canal company engaged five additional contractors to work on the project; this brought about a more consistent progress and although further problems of a geological nature presented themselves, by the summer of 1788 the tunnel was essentially complete. In that same year, George III, who was convalescing at Cheltenham, went with members of the Royal Family to visit the Earl of

Bathurst and were taken to see the eastern and western portals of the tunnel, which gave them cause for much astonishment.

On completion of the work, Josiah Clowes found the floor of the tunnel not as level as he would have wished, and though he was being pressed by the canal company to water the tunnel, he considered this action to be premature. He nevertheless conceded their request and joined by others he made a passage through the tunnel in April 1789. But he found the finish was not as perfect as he would have liked: from the Daneway portal the tunnel passed through Fuller's earth which required lining with brick and stone, and as it entered into inferior oolite the blasting charges had enlarged sections beyond the specified height and width; as it passed again through Fuller's earth a geological fault had been encountered and finally as it entered the great oolite, walling and arching needed attention, the latter having been skimped by reducing the required three rings of brick-work to only one ring. Although it was not a cause of faulty workmanship, leakage at times was suffiently bad that in 1790 it was necessary to close the tunnel for three months to allow remedial work to be carried out, including the renewal of some of the clay lining. But the leakage persisted and Robert Mylne was asked by the canal company for an opinion, and in the following year the tunnel was again closed so that remedial work could be undertaken.

From the Coates portal the canal passed through rocky ground which Robert Whitworth described as the worse he had seen for a canal of such length, particularly as there was a tendency for the area to remain dry outside the months of winter. These conditions made it necessary for the bed of the canal to have a double lining comprising a two foot puddle of clay and above that a two foot trodden layer of clay; but as it turned out, the work undertaken by the contractor was skimped.

The summit level of the canal extended to within one and a quarter miles of Cirencester where there was a branch to the town, while the main line continued to Siddington where four locks began the descent that eventually led to the Thames. The Siddington locks together with a further eleven locks brought the canal to Inglesham by way of Cerney Wick, Latton (where there was a junction with the North Wiltshire canal), Marston Meysey and Kempsford. But before the canal was joined with the Thames, boats had already started to carry coal to Kempsford, and it was not until late November 1789 that boats passed through Inglesham lock and on to the Thames. Once they had done so, their continuing passage downstream was fraught with difficulties, though trade was established at new wharves at Lechlade where Staffordshire coal was unloaded in late

December. And though the trade in coal increased, through traffic to Oxford and London was not a light undertaking and this situation prevailed until January 1792.

The unsatisfactory state of the upper Thames was not only hindering river trade along its route, but it was affecting the lower regions of the river as well. Hence the Thames Navigation Committee of the Corporation of London, who had undertaken major improvements to the river below Staines, decided to see for themselves how trade was affected by the condition of the canal and the upper Thames. In 1816 they arrived at Brinscombe Port and passed along the canal to Inglesham. On their journey they noted leaking lock gates and instances of water leaking from the banks of the canal. Their comments, which they passed on to the canal company, did little good and only routine maintenance was carried out until 1820 when the shortage of water in the canal had become so acute that the canal company sought the advice of a well known firm of contractors. They inspected the canal between Stroud and Latton and recommended that areas of the summit pound be relined with the best clay available. Many of the locks were overhauled and to avoid wasting water, side ponds were built at certain locks. The action of these ponds was to take a third or more of the water from the lock as it emptied, and then to store it until the lock was refilled. Later, in 1831, Wilmoreway lower lock was provided with a side pond as it drew too much water from the upper pound each time it was used; a situation that may not have occurred if the supply from the Boxwell springs had been in accordance with expectations.

It must be concluded as regrettable that the canal reached a peak in traffic figures at a time when the threat of the railways became a reality. With the eventual decline in revenues, the proprietors proposed on two occasions to convert the canal into a railway. Although this did not happen, there followed a period of indirect control by railway companies and that was followed by a county council management scheme.

No doubt the mixed ownership of the canal did not help matters and it was not until 1895 that the Great Western Railway transferred its shareholding to a joint venture comprising five navigation authorities and six public bodies, namely, the Thames and Severn Canal Trust which was incorporated by an Act (Victoria) of 1895. The Trust was in a position to borrow £15,000 to put the canal in good order and they hoped that the flow of through traffic to Oxford would be helped by improvements to the upper Thames navigation by the Thames Conservancy, work that had in fact started in 1892 and carried on until 1898.

It is difficult to envisage how the sum of £15,000 would be sufficient to rectify the many defects the canal had presented over the past hundred years, and as it turned out a further loan was needed before the canal was fully opened in March 1899. But the summer that followed brought about the same old problems of insufficient water and leakage at the summit level, a matter that had been commented upon the previous year in the December issue of *The Engineer* which stated that 'it is doubtful whether there is any portion of canal in England more troublesome to keep water-tight than this [summit level] has been'.

As the Trust had failed to keep the canal in a satisfactory condition, they approached the Gloucestershire County Council who were a major contributor of funds to the Trust and proposed that the Council should take on the management of the canal. First, the chairman of the Council engaged a reliable and experienced engineer to prepare an estimate for treating the leaking summit level. He then persuaded the councillors in January 1900 to obtain a warrant from the Board of Trade giving the Trust authority to abandon the canal on the grounds that it was derelict, and then to apply for a provisional order to transfer the canal to the care of the County Council. It is not unusual that county councils make errors of judgement and in this instance the judgement of the Gloucestershire County Council to take on the management of a canal with a history of engineering faults and poor workmanship in its building, was unfortunate to say the least. However, the Council were not in a position to proceed until the summer of 1901 when they formed a management committee and engaged a young civil engineer who took the trouble to talk to those who had known the canal for many years and who had worked upon it, and from what they said to him he was able to work out that a major problem presented itself at the summit level east of the tunnel. It was here that the bottom of the canal was undermined by a complexity of springs for about 450yd. He therefore proposed lining this stretch of canal with concrete and taking water away from the springs by pipes, a procedure that turned out to be successful. Next, the management committee considered re-puddling the remainder of the summit level that followed the concreted section. The county councillors, faced with this additional expenditure to make the summit level completely watertight, could see only too well where all this was leading, but they finally though reluctantly agreed to the re-puddling work. Yet again the work was skimped, even though the contractor's men worked for nine months, during which time the summit level was unnavigable. Added to all this, more work had to be carried out on the tunnel and extensive dredging was undertaken by a steam operated dredger that the management committee had purchased specifically to work on the canal. Gradually the canal was re-opened, section by section, though it was not until January 1904 that the entire summit level was navigable.

In 1895 the Thames and Severn Canal Trust had been limited to borrowing £15,000, though nine years later that sum had doubled and it was not until March 1904 that the first delivery of coal for sixteen years was unloaded at the wharf at Cirencester. It would appear that a new phase in trade was about to take place, but this was not to be and the years that followed saw a decline in usage of the canal between Chalford and Inglesham. Continued leakages and a shortage of water brought about temporary closures which finally determined the abandonment of that part of the canal.

And so it was in April 1911 that the last boat carrying grain passed through to Lechlade aided by the pumping of additional water into the summit level to give sufficient depth for the laden vessel. In the last days of the month that followed, the last vessel to navigate the full length of the canal reached Inglesham; it was the *Flower of Gloster*.

STROUD TO INGLESHAM

As the *Flower of Gloster* approached Brinscombe Port the land either side of the canal became 'studded with the grey Gloucestershire houses', the blue slate roofs of the houses and mills offsetting the golden aura of the valley. Temple Thurston saw pasture that had been left untouched, the grass a golden green, accentuated by areas of cowslip. Shortly after Chalford the houses became less frequent and the wooded sides of the valley began to rise as the canal ascended; as did the river Frome which wound alongside the course of the canal and had been vital in supplying water to drive the mills in the valley. Soon he saw only the occasional stray farm or lock house representing human habitation and he signalled to Eynsham Harry to stop so that he could investigate the nearby woods. He counted seventeen varieties of wild flower: purple orchis amongst bluebells, cuckoo-pint, veronica, primroses, violets and ground ivy, and king-cups with sepals richly golden, and lesser celandine and others. And shading these flowers the leaves of countless trees in the flush of spring.

As he left the woods he could only stand and wonder what man would say if by magic he was wafted from the streets of a grey city to the Golden Valley. But while he was away in the woods, Eynsham Harry had prepared a speciality dish for their lunch. 'I be waiting for you to taste that dish, sur,' he said. Temple Thurston viewed the dish of green vegetable that looked like spinach, and trying it, declared that it was better than asparagus. Eynsham Harry explained: 'There be hops growing up on that hedge, sur; these that you're eating be the young shoots, cut off about six inches from the top and boiled the same as other greens.' Temple Thurston thought he would remember the dish when next May came, though he doubted he would find a hedge in London where the wild hop-vine grows.

As they progressed toward the summit level of the canal they passed Baker's mill and the site of Puck mill with Tanner's wood to their left. At Whitehall bridge the dense areas of Frampton wood to their right and Siccaridge wood to their left were more extensive than in the lower valley. The locks that had been far apart became more frequent, starting with Bathurst's Meadow lock and ending with Wharf lock adjacent to the Daneway basin just below Daneway bridge.

Throughout their journey from Stroud they had passed only one boat, an old lady at the tiller wearing a 'capaciouse barge bonnet' and seeming perfectly able to manage the more difficult parts of the navigation. Although the locks were in good condition, the water level in the pounds was low, providing barely sufficient depth to keep the *Flower of Gloster* afloat, and this made extra work for Fanny the horse. In one short pound the water was so low that two young boys were bathing and areas of luxuriant weed could be seen below the surface of the water.

Just beyond Daneway bridge stands the Bricklayers' Arms and opposite the inn was Summit lock which has long since been filled in and acts as a car park for the inn. Nearby is Daneway House which was occupied by the craftsman and designer Ernest Gimson and used as his workshop and showroom. The Barnsley brothers, Ernest and Sidney, were also part of the arts and craft movement at Sapperton and it was Ernest who, primarily an architect (his brother was more concerned with furniture making), built three houses and the Village Hall, which was completed in 1913; but his most notable work was Rodmarton Manor near Cirencester, perhaps the crowning achievement of arts and crafts architecture in the Cotswolds. During his visit to the Bricklayer's Arms, Temple Thurston talked to an old man whose grandfather had met the King on the towing path leading to the Coates portal when George III and his entourage came to see the wonder of Sapperton tunnel. The man's grandfather was given a sovereign by the King and when he compared the likeness on the coin with the giver he knew it really was the King who had spoken to him.

As the *Flower of Gloster* entered the tunnel at the Daneway portal, Temple Thurston felt a sense of real adventure. No doubt Eynsham Harry had arranged with a local lad to take Fanny overland to the other end of

The church of St Kenelm, Sapperton, where in the graveyard are buried Ernest Gimson and Ernest and Sidney Barnsley, major figures in the arts and craft movement at Sapperton.

The remains of Red Lion lock in the Golden Valley. Although the walls of the lock chamber are intact, the gates have long since disappeared. This scene of dereliction is typical of the locks leading up through the valley to Daneway.

The Coates portal of Sapperton tunnel was restored by the Cotswold Canals Trust
in 1977. In its former dilapidated state, much of the original masonry was found
lying in the canal bed and only a little new stone was needed during restoration.

The Thames & Severn canal Roundhouse at Cerney Wick seen from the towing path. During the summer months, growth in the dried out bed of the canal is abundant.

the tunnel, while he and Temple Thurston started to leg their way through. He asked Eynsham Harry what a professional legger would have been paid during the heyday of the canal: five shillings for a loaded boat and half that sum for an empty one, was Harry's reply. 'A pound wouldn't satisfy me,' was Temple Thurston's comment. 'No, sur, I suspect not.' replied Harry. 'It's always easier to do these things for nothing.' As they left the tunnel it was evening and though the sun had set, the light seemed dazzling after the long hours of darkness they had endured.

Their journey was nearing its end and following an overnight stop they passed through the locks at Siddington and the junction with the North Wiltshire canal at Latton. But a little before Latton, at Cerney Wick, they passed one of the five roundhouses which were occupied by the lengthmen who kept the canal in order. Just as most of the unique barrel vaulted canal-side cottages on the Stratford canal have fallen into private hands and suffered unsympathetic alterations, a similar situation has occurred with some of the roundhouses.[1] But the roundhouse at Cerney Wick has suffered less, and even though it had fallen into disuse it was sold at auction in 1963 for £250 and used as a weekend retreat by a student nurse and her friends. There was neither electricity nor running water, though there was a well and a privy in the garden. Over the years the property was improved but the peaceful seclusion it once enjoyed became eroded as the main road between Cirencester and Swindon carried increasingly more traffic.

As they passed through the village of Kempsford they met a lengthman who was working at keeping the towing path clear of overhanging bushes, even though he had not seen a boat for at least six weeks before the *Flower of Gloster*. It was not long before the *Flower of Gloster* entered the canal basin at Inglesham and the tow-rope sagged loose in the water. It was the end of Temple Thurston's journey of discovery and he bade Eynsham Harry goodbye and started to make his way across a meadow in the direction of Lechlade. He looked back and saw that Eynsham Harry had already turned the *Flower of Gloster* in the basin and was hitching Fanny to the tow-rope as he made preparations for returning the boat to Coventry and its owner Joseph Phipkin. From there he would return to his own boat, the *Henrietta*, named after his wife and moored at Hillmorton near Rugby.

1. Inglesham lock and roundhouse were acquired in 2002 by British Waterways in anticipation of the future restoration of the Thames and Severn canal.

10

THE PAST, THE PRESENT AND THE FUTURE

Temple Thurston ended his journey at Inglesham as he had no more time at his disposal; and it was necessary that Eynsham Harry and the *Flower of Gloster* return to Coventry as the boat was needed by its owner. And in any case, the journey on to Oxford would have depended upon the navigable condition of the upper Thames, which was far from perfect and the old flash weir at Eaton Hastings was then an impediment to navigation. It is as well therefore to consider what the *Flower of Gloster* may have encountered had it continued on its journey.

The history of navigation on the upper Thames dates back to the time when the cutting of the Thames and Severn canal was within a few miles of Inglesham and the Thames Navigation Commissioners were delaying building locks that were essential to the navigable state of the river between Inglesham and Oxford. Just as it was essential that the Thames and Severn Canal Company wanted easy access to Oxford and beyond, it was equally essential that the Thames Commissioners were convinced that the canal would provide sufficient volume of through traffic to make the cost of building locks worthwhile. At almost the last moment, the Commissioners went ahead with a programme of improvements to the upper Thames in accordance with the recommendations made by William Jessop, although a little later, Robert Mylne, who was asked for an opinion on the state of the river following the work that had been carried out, was not convinced that the locks proposed by Jessop were sufficient for ease of navigation, and he proposed building further locks. Mylne was also critical of the canal and the trade it was estimated it would create.

But it was because of the failure of the Commissioners to implement Mylne's additional improvements to the river and the subsequent navigational difficulties, that the Thames and Severn Canal Company finally joined up with the Wiltshire and Berkshire canal, which enabled traffic to leave the Thames and Severn canal at Latton and enter the

Part of the lock chamber and bridge at the end of the Thames & Severn canal at Inglesham. Although the chamber of the lock is overgrown, the infilled section of canal between the lock and the river Thames was excavated in 2003, letting water come up to the lock in anticipation of future restoration work. The Inglesham Roundhouse is out of picture to the right.

The Thames at Inglesham looking up stream. Dead centre of picture is the entrance to the Thames & Severn canal which is now cleared as far as the lock. Left of centre is the partly overgrown Roundhouse.

Thames at Abingdon by way of the North Wiltshire canal. In this way, traffic bypassed the upper Thames. This led to a loss of trade between Lechlade and Oxford and when the newly appointed Conservators of the River Thames arranged for their superintendent of the upper river to carry out a survey in 1866, he found the river virtually unnavigable. Ironically, the final years of through traffic on the Thames and Severn canal about the turn of the century coincided with a period of improvement on the upper river that more or less followed the recommendations made by Mylne a hundred years earlier. Even so, it was not until 1928 when the Thames Conservancy built Eynsham and King's locks and in 1937 removed the flash weir at Eaton Hastings that the upper Thames became a more acceptable navigation.

Today, the improvements that have been made to the canals and rivers Temple Thurston navigated make all but one part of his journey straightforward and without impediment. The present stumbling block that prevents Temple Thurston's journey from being completed to Inglesham, is the partly derelict Thames and Severn canal. But over the past years the Cotswold Canals Trust has been active in preventing further deterioration of this important waterway. The Trust has been engaged in rebuilding certain locks and bridges, clearing towing paths and making preparation for the hoped for rebuilding of the entire canal, a project that is currently being assessed. Should this reconstruction work be undertaken, future canal enthusiasts will have before them one of the most fascinating canal and river journeys in England. And should the former canal basin at Oxford, that is now a car park, be reconstituted, the traveller will be able to leave from almost the same spot that Temple Thurston started his journey in 1911, and return by way of the upper Thames and Isis lock.

APPENDIX

Map of Temple Thurston's Journey